TIME
FOR KIDS

Snakes
Up Close

Christopher Blazeman

Consultant

Timothy Rasinski, Ph.D.
Kent State University

Publishing Credits

Dona Herweck Rice, *Editor-in-Chief*
Robin Erickson, *Production Director*
Lee Aucoin, *Creative Director*
Conni Medina, M.A.Ed., *Editorial Director*
Jamey Acosta, *Editor*
Stephanie Reid, *Photo Editor*
Rachelle Cracchiolo, M.S.Ed., *Publisher*

Based on writing from *TIME For Kids.*

TIME For Kids and the *TIME For Kids* logo are registered trademarks of TIME Inc. Used under license.

Teacher Created Materials

5301 Oceanus Drive
Huntington Beach, CA 92649-1030
http://www.tcmpub.com

ISBN 978-1-4333-3618-8

© 2012 by Teacher Created Materials, Inc.

Table of Contents

Sammy 4

All About Snakes 8

How Snakes Live 16

Snake Chart 27

Glossary 28

Sammy

"Mom, can I keep him?" you ask.

"Keep who?" she says.

"Sammy," you answer.

"Who is Sammy?" she asks.

"Sssssss," Sammy hisses.

"Ahhhh!" Mom screams.

So, who is Sammy?

Sammy is a snake, of course!

python

Would a snake make a good pet? This book will tell you about snakes. When you finish, you can decide for yourself. But be sure you ask before you bring one home!

All About Snakes

albino python

orange python

Some snakes are as long as a tree. Some are as short as a finger. Some are thick, and some are thin. Some are dangerous, but most are harmless.

boa constrictor

grass snake

Snakes can be different. But
they are the same in many ways,
too.

9

Snakes are reptiles. Most snakes lay tough, leathery eggs. When a baby snake is born, it does not need its mother's care. It can take care of itself.

Scales cover the bodies
of snakes. They look wet and
slimy, but they are really dry and
hard.

Snakes have no legs. They must glide on their bellies or wiggle from side to side.

Snakes have no eyelids. No problem! They have a thin layer that protects their eyes.

Snakes do not have ears. They feel movement on the ground. That is their way of hearing.

Can snakes smell? Yes, with the help of their forked tongues!

forked tongue

corn snake

coral snake

diamondback
rattlesnake

Snakes are **cold blooded**.
Their body heat depends on
the heat around them. That is
why most snakes live in warm
places.

How Snakes Live

Even so, you can find snakes everywhere. Snakes may live in jungles, swamps, forests, and deserts.

They may live in trees, lakes, or holes in the ground.

Even if you do not know where a snake lives, you can tell where one has been. Snakes shed their skin as they grow.

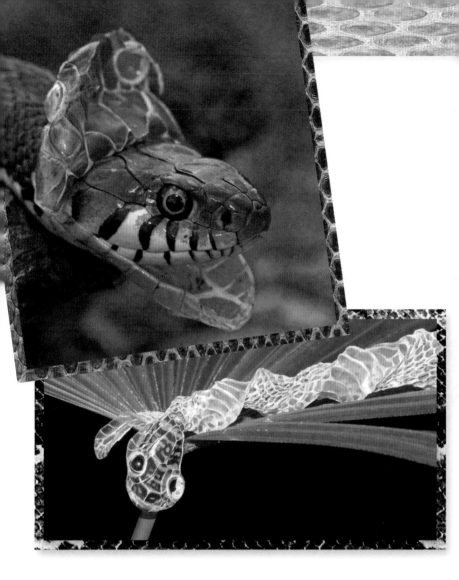

The skin peels off like a sock.
Then the snake crawls away,
leaving its skin behind.

rattlesnake

rattle

Sometimes snakes let you
know where they are. They may
rattle their tails or make noises
to frighten you away.

green
mamba

albino
cobra

Some snakes play dead to
protect themselves. Others have
bright colors to show that they
are poisonous.

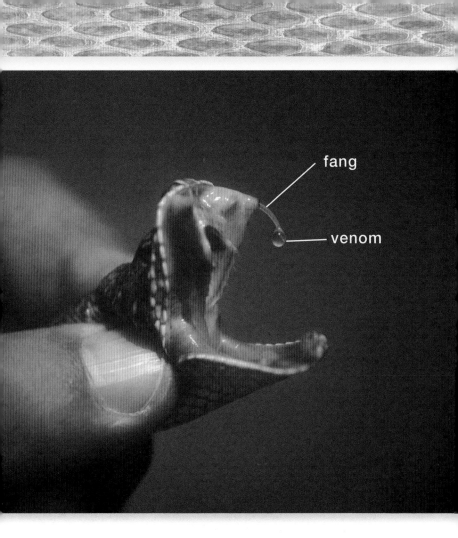

fang

venom

Snake poison is called **venom**. Venom flows through the hollow, sharp **fangs** of some snakes. They use venom to stop other animals.

Since all snakes eat meat, venom helps some of them get their food. Others **squeeze** their food until it dies.

Snakes swallow their food whole. Sometimes it is even still alive!

Usually snakes eat small animals. Some snakes have **hinges** on their jaws to open wide and eat large animals, too.

So, will a snake make a good pet? There is no right answer. You must decide for yourself.

To help you decide, here is a chart to remind you all about snakes.

SNAKE CHART

eyes	two eyes but no eyelids
ears	no ears, so they feel movement around them
bodies	covered with scales, have no legs, are cold blooded, and shed skin
movement	glide or wiggle
babies	hatch from eggs or born live; can take care of themselves
protection	rattle, make noises, play dead, have bright colors, or spit venom
eating	bite or squeeze and swallow whole
living place	jungles, swamps, forests, trees, lakes, holes in the ground, or tanks

Glossary

cold blooded—having body heat that depends on the heat around you

fangs—long, pointed teeth

hinges—joints that allow snakes to open their jaws very wide

scales—hard, dry plates that cover the bodies of snakes

squeeze—to crush tightly; for snakes, this is also called *constriction*

venom—poison that flows through the hollow fangs of some snakes